JUNGLE
ADVENTURES

By Camilla Gersh

Series Editor Deborah Lock
Project Editor Camilla Gersh
Editors Caryn Jenner, Pomona Zaheer
Project Art Editor Hoa Luc
Design Assistant Emma Hobson
Art Editor Yamini Panwar
Producer, Pre-Production Francesca Wardell
Illustrator Hoa Luc
DTP Designers Anita Yadav, Vijay Kandwal
Picture Researcher Sakshi Saluja
Managing Editor Soma B. Chowdhury
Managing Art Editor Ahlawat Gunjan

Reading Consultant
Shirley Bickler
Subject Consultant
David Emmett, Conservation International

With special thanks to Amy van Nice,
Wildlife Alliance

First published in Great Britain in 2015 by
Dorling Kindersley Limited
80 Strand, London, WC2R 0RL

Copyright © 2015 Dorling Kindersley Limited
A Penguin Random House Company
15 16 17 18 19 10 9 8 7 6 5 4 3 2 1
001—271069—April/15

A CIP catalogue record for this book
is available from the British Library.
ISBN: 978-0-2411-8274-1

Printed and bound in China

The publisher would like to thank the following for their kind permission to reproduce their photographs:
(Key: a-above; b-below/bottom; c-centre; f-far; l-left; r-right; t-top)

1 Alamy Images: Daniel Santacatalina Laborda. 6–7 Dreamstime.com: Pixelalex. 8 Getty Images: Thomas Barwick/Stone. 10 Getty Images: webphotographeer/
E+. 15 Alamy Images: Alexey Gnilenkov. 17 Alamy Images: Zoonar/Vladimir Blinov. 18 Alamy Images: Gustav Gonget/G&B Images. 20 Alamy Images: Bradley
Ireland/Danita Delimont, Agent. 23 Getty Images: Ricardo Reitmeyer/E+. 24 Dreamstime.com: Irochka (cl); Andrey Sukhachev (br). 25 Dreamstime.com:
Dannyphoto80 (br); Peter Wollinga (cl). 31 Alamy Images: Michael Stubblefield. 32 Alamy Images: mediacolor's. 34 Alamy Images: Kjersti Joergensen.
37 David Emmett, Conservation International. 38 Alamy Images: Daniel Santacatalina Laborda (l). 39 David Emmett, Conservation International: (br).
40 Alamy Images: Bill Attwell (bl); Joe McDonald/Steve Bloom Images (cl). 41 Alamy Images: Ganesh H Shankar (tl); Henry Westheim Photography (br).
Dorling Kindersley: Whipsnade Zoo, Bedfordshire (crb). 43 Corbis: 145/Don Farrall/Ocean (bl). 45 Alamy Images: Pawel Bienkowski. 46 Getty Images: Mark
Carwardine/Photolibrary. 47 Alamy Images: Ginette Peach. 48 Alamy Images: Yvette Cardozo. 50–51 Alamy Images: Tim Gainey. 51 David Emmett,
Conservation International: (br). 52 David Emmett, Conservation International: (bl, br). 53 David Emmett, Conservation International: (clb, br). 54 Alamy
Images: Sam Yue (c). 58 Alamy Images: Gavriel Jecan/Danita Delimont, Agent (cl); blickwinkel/Layer (cra); komkrit tonusin (crb). 59 Alamy Images: Peter
Newton (tl). Getty Images: Paul Kennedy/Lonely Planet Images (cl). naturepl.com: Nick Garbutt (cr). 61 Getty Images: Danita Delimont/Gallo Images.
62 Koulang Chey, Conservation International. 63 David Emmett, Conservation International. 65 Alamy Images: ZUMA Press, Inc.. 66 Alamy Images:
Wayne Neal. 69 David Emmett, Conservation International: (t, br). 76 Getty Images: Peter Charlesworth / LightRocket. 79 David Emmett,
Conservation International: (br). 81 Alamy Images: Atlaspix. 84–85 David Emmett, Conservation International.
86–87 Dreamstime.com: Lightzoom (b). 88 Alamy Images: Anders Blomqvist. 89 David Emmett, Conservation International. 90 Corbis: ZSSD/Minden
Pictures. 92–93 Getty Images: Steve Winter/National Geographic. 94 Getty Images: Caroline Schiff/The Image Bank. 96 Alamy Images: dpa picture alliance
archive. 99 Dreamstime.com: Jiripravda (tl); Riyanto Samui Daja (br). 100 Corbis: 13/Martin Harvey/Ocean (br). 101 Corbis: Shin Yoshino/Minden Pictures (tr).
103 David Emmett, Conservation International. 105 Alamy Images: Paul Kingsley. 106–107 Alamy Images: David Davis Photoproductions RF.
108–109 Alamy Images: Thailand Wildlife. 110 David Emmett, Conservation International. 111 David Emmett, Conservation International: (br).
114–115 Alamy Images: Pawel Bienkowski. 114 Wildlife Alliance: Amy Van (c). 115 Alamy Images: Terry Whittaker (cla, cl, cr, crb).
117 Corbis: Philip Lee Harvey. 118–119 Corbis: Yi Lu/Viewstock. 120 Dorling Kindersley: Jamie Marshall (bc). 120–121 Dorling Kindersley:
Bethany Dawn. 121 Dorling Kindersley: Tim Draper/Rough Guides (tl); Bethany Dawn (cb).
Jacket images: Front: Getty Images: Tom Brakefield; Back: Corbis: Yi Lu/Viewstock (tl); Spine: David Emmett, Conservation International: (b).

All other images © Dorling Kindersley Limited
For further information see: www.dkimages.com

A WORLD OF IDEAS:
SEE ALL THERE IS TO KNOW

www.dk.com

Contents

Location

Deep in the humid mountain forests of Cambodia lies a mysterious world filled with rare and undiscovered animals. Here a group of dedicated explorers begins a journey to uncover the secrets of the Cardamom Mountains.

Cambodia

■ Siem Reap

Mekong River

▲ Cardamom Mountains

★ Phnom Penh

Prek Tnort River

Koh Kong

Southeast Asia

Andaman Sea

Gulf of
Thailand

Expedition Team

The deepest forests of the Cardamom Mountains are a place where few humans venture, but our team is on a mission. Each member is a specialist looking for a particular type of animal.

PHRUN KEO
Mammalogist (mammal expert)

ROBIN BEAK
Ornithologist (bird expert)

LIZ TERRAPIN
Herpetologist (reptile and amphibian expert)

PHHOUNG SUY
Herpetologist (reptile and amphibian expert)

FINN HERRING
Ichthyologist (fish expert)

ANTHONY BUGG
Entomologist (insect expert)

SEYHA DITH
Arachnologist (spider expert)

BOPHA SIN
Botanist (plant expert)

CHARLOTTE COOK
Student

KIRI KHLOT
Guide

Prologue

Charlotte flinched as the nurse stuck a needle into her arm. "That's one," the nurse said, smiling widely. "Only a few more to go." She winked at her patient. Charlotte returned a crooked smile and sighed as she tried to distract herself by looking around the nurse's spotless white office.

"So, is this your first trip to Cambodia?" the nurse continued. Charlotte nodded.

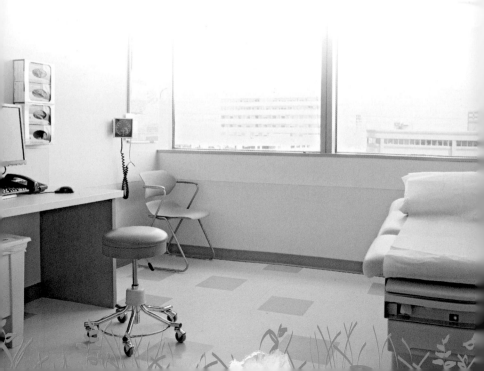

"Do you do much travelling?" the nurse asked, trying to make conversation.

"No. Actually, this is the first time I've ever left the country," Charlotte replied.

"How exciting!" the nurse said. "Pretty exotic place for your first trip abroad. Are you going on holiday?"

"Nope. Research," Charlotte replied. "Ow!" she exclaimed as the nurse jabbed a shot into her other arm.

"Sorry. Research?"

"Mm-hmm. Into animals. We're trying to count how many different types we see and how many there are of each type. It's called a biodiversity survey."

"Wow. So does that mean you have to spend a lot of time in the jungle?"

Charlotte gazed at her, frowned and took a deep breath. "Yeah."

"Sounds like fun! You don't seem too excited about it, though."

"Well, I'm not crazy about camping," she said.

The nurse shrugged. "I guess sleeping on cold, wet ground isn't for everyone. I bet there'll be snakes, too! Hope you don't get any creepy-crawlies in your sleeping bag!"

As soon as the words 'creepy-crawlies' came out of the nurse's mouth, images of flies, spiders and… cockroaches began to crawl through Charlotte's mind. She began to feel dizzy, and then the nurse said, "Are you feeling OK? You look a little pale. Don't worry – that was the last shot. You're all done."

It was not the shots Charlotte was thinking about, though. It was the cockroaches in her sleeping bag!

"So if you don't like camping, why are you going on the trip?" the nurse asked.

Charlotte started to feel better once her mind was directed towards other thoughts.

"I love animals – apart from the creepy ones. I've loved big cats as long as I can remember. They're so beautiful! I want to help take care of them, and this trip is going to help me learn how, so it's worth putting up with bugs."

"Oh! Well I guess you'll have to get used to sleeping outside then."

Charlotte really hoped she could.

Camping Gear Checklist

You will need lots of equipment if you are going to spend a long time in the jungle. Don't leave home without this essential gear.

CHECKLIST

- [x] A first aid kit is vital for any cuts, scrapes or illness. Make sure none of the medicine is out-of-date.

- [x] A clothes-washing kit should contain a bowl or bucket, detergent and gloves.

- [x] A wash kit will have small bottles of soap, shampoo, hand sanitiser and anything else you need.

- [x] A compass will help you find your way.

- [x] Waterproof bags have infinite uses but are especially handy for keeping clothes dry and for storing dirty clothes.

- [x] Clotheslines are essential for leaving your clothes out to dry.

- [x] A pocketknife can be used for lots of small jobs, from cutting rope to extracting fishhooks.

WITH A BACKPACK, ORGANISATION AND EASY ACCESS ARE KEY. USE THESE BASIC PACKING TIPS AS A GUIDE.

Store essentials such as sunblock, a compass, maps and guidebooks in an outer pocket.

Pack rain gear at the top where you can get it quickly.

Keep first aid items accessible.

Heaviest items should sit between your shoulder blades and as close to your back as possible.

Waterproof bags should be used to store items that must stay dry, particularly spare clothing.

Carry your water bottle upright, where it is always accessible.

Lighter items should remain at the bottom of the backpack.

Store fuel bottles upright and outside the pack.

CHAPTER 1
Welcome to the Jungle

THUMP, THUMP, THUMP. The van started making strange noises just as it exited the city limits of Phnom Penh, the capital of Cambodia.

"Hmm. Sounds like a flat," said Liz. She was Charlotte's mentor and would take care of her on the expedition.

The driver pulled over, and everyone climbed out of the van to see. Sure enough, the front left tyre was flat. Liz helped the driver change the tyre, while Charlotte waited with the other passengers she had just met: Robin, a bird expert; Finn, a fish specialist; and Phrun, a mammal expert. They would all be travelling together to Koh Kong and joining the expedition there.

Soon the new tyre was on, and they were ready to hit the road again. The group chatted in the van on the way.

"Let's hope we see lots of rare species out there," Robin said. "According to reports, the numbers are down this year in Cambodia. It's really very worrying."

Charlotte recalled what Liz had said when she was thinking of signing up. "We won't know which animals are in trouble unless we know how many are out there."

Back in the van, Liz responded to Robin's comment, "But the Cardamom Mountains are so poorly understood and explored. There could be thousands of species there that we've never even heard about. Maybe we'll even get to see some animals we thought were gone forever."

Charlotte knew that Liz was thinking of the Siamese crocodile, which had long been thought to be extinct – to have died out completely. It had only recently been rediscovered in the Cardamom Mountains, and Liz was hoping to see it for herself. For her part, Charlotte hoped that she would get to see a tiger.

The group continued without a word for about half an hour, when Finn broke the silence. "Check it out. We're following the Prek Tnort River. It flows into the great Mekong, the lifeline for almost all of Southeast Asia. According to legend, the great Naga – a giant, snake-like creature – lives in the Mekong. Some years back, they discovered a new species of giant catfish living in the river – it really was a whopper! In fact, it's the world's largest freshwater fish! Lots of people think that this must be where the stories came from, but I like to believe that the Naga is still out there."

After a few hours of chit-chat and stories, Charlotte and her stomach were relieved when they finally arrived in Koh Kong. The bumpy, winding roads were getting to be a bit much for the both of them.

In Koh Kong, they met Kiri Khlot, their guide to the Cardamoms. Also waiting for them was a helicopter, which had been lent to them for the journey. The propellers were already rotating, ready for takeoff.

"This is going to be great," Phrun said. "I love these things! Don't you?" he continued as he leapt into the helicopter enthusiastically before Charlotte even had a chance to respond.

Charlotte eyed the helicopter warily as everyone else proceeded to board. Soon she and Liz were the only ones left. Liz grabbed Charlotte by the arm and, dragging her towards the helicopter, said, "Hey, I'm not crazy about these things either, but it's the best way to get to where we're going. There aren't many roads in the part of the forest we're visiting. Don't worry. It's pretty safe. Our pilot has years of experience."

Charlotte cautiously boarded the helicopter, strapped herself in, and put on the headset that Liz handed her. The helicopter lifted off the ground, rocking slightly. Charlotte gripped the armrests tightly. The helicopter steadied as it raised itself high above the trees before moving off away from the helipad.

Charlotte began to relax and then noticed smoke rising up in steady streams from the land below. Liz noticed that Charlotte's eyes were fixed on the view out of the window, and then Charlotte heard Liz's voice coming through the headset. "They're using the slash-and-burn technique. When local people need to clear land for farming, they cut down all the trees and burn whatever's left – branches, leaves, stumps and even the tree trunks. It makes the ground fertile in the short term, but it's extremely harmful to the forest, the animals that live in it and the air around. It can also permanently damage the soil."

For the next few minutes, there was silence in the cabin; the only sounds were the whirring of the helicopter blades and the hum of the motor. Then, out of nowhere, the skies opened up and there came a tremendous downpour. The heavy rains were accompanied by terrible winds, and the helicopter began to list and rock from side to side. Charlotte was certain the helicopter was going to crash, so she squeezed her eyes shut, expecting these to be her final moments on Earth. At that second, she felt a sudden jerk, and the helicopter stopped moving.

"Is that it? Am I dead?" she thought to herself. She opened her eyes to see that she and everyone else were still sitting strapped into the helicopter.

Suddenly Phrun said, "Woohoo! That was incredible! That was the best helicopter ride ever!"

They had landed. Charlotte was relieved to be safe on solid ground. One by one, the team and crew exited the helicopter. All around them were pitcher plants, orchids with yellow flowers and long stems and soft, spongy moss. There were also lush green plants as far as the eye could see, and it was still raining.

"Are we there?" she asked Liz.

"No, I'm afraid we're still miles from where we want to be. We'll have to go the rest of the way on foot."

Charlotte let out an audible groan, and Liz eyed her with raised eyebrows. Embarrassed, Charlotte tried to avoid eye contact with her by gazing around at the fleshy vegetation. Then she heard a rustling sound, as if something was moving in the bushes. She stared deeply into the greenery and saw a pair of large yellow eyes gazing back at her.

Taxonomy of Living Things

To help us understand how life-forms on the planet are related to one another, scientists organise them into six large groups called kingdoms. This classification is called taxonomy.

PLANTS

Plants are complex, multicelled organisms that can make their own food. They include mosses, conifers and flowering plants.

EUBACTERIA

These are simple, single-celled bacteria. This type of bacteria can cause diseases or turn milk into yoghurt.

ARCHAEOBACTERIA

These simple, single-celled bacteria are thought to be among the oldest living things on the planet. They can survive in hostile environments, such as boiling water.

ANIMALS

Animals range from the very simple, such as a sponge, to the highly complex, such as mammals and humans.

FUNGI

Mushrooms, moulds and yeasts are all fungi. Fungi gain their energy by breaking down dead plants and animals.

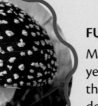

PROTISTS

Protists include amoebae, slime moulds, algae and protozoa. They are microscopic single-celled organisms, and each species is different.

Global Warming and Deforestation

Destroying forests has a major impact on our planet. Studying the diversity of animals in a given area (its biodiversity) provides clues as to how the planet is doing. This chart shows what can happen if forests are destroyed.

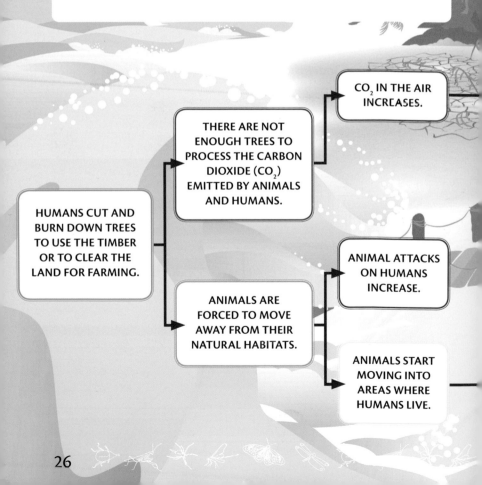

HUMANS CUT AND BURN DOWN TREES TO USE THE TIMBER OR TO CLEAR THE LAND FOR FARMING.

THERE ARE NOT ENOUGH TREES TO PROCESS THE CARBON DIOXIDE (CO_2) EMITTED BY ANIMALS AND HUMANS.

CO_2 IN THE AIR INCREASES.

ANIMALS ARE FORCED TO MOVE AWAY FROM THEIR NATURAL HABITATS.

ANIMAL ATTACKS ON HUMANS INCREASE.

ANIMALS START MOVING INTO AREAS WHERE HUMANS LIVE.

THE SUN'S LIGHT BECOMES TRAPPED IN THE ATMOSPHERE MORE EASILY, CAUSING GLOBAL TEMPERATURES TO INCREASE.

WEATHER PATTERNS CHANGE.

EXTREME WEATHER, SUCH AS BLIZZARDS, DROUGHTS AND HURRICANES, BECOMES WIDESPREAD.

POLAR ICE CAPS MELT AND SEA LEVEL RISES.

FLOODING BECOMES MORE COMMON, AND THERE IS THE POSSIBILITY THAT COASTAL COMMUNITIES MAY BE SWALLOWED BY THE SEA.

ANIMALS HAVE TROUBLE FINDING FOOD AND MIGHT STARVE.

SPECIES BECOME EXTINCT.

THE MYSTERIOUS NAGA

BORN FROM THE NAGA

Cambodians sometimes say that they are 'born from the Naga'. In Cambodian legend, the Naga were a race of reptiles, and the Cambodian people are descendants of the marriage between the Naga king's daughter and the king of ancient Cambodia.

NAGA SYMBOL

Naga are familiar symbols in many Southeast Asian countries. They symbolise prosperity and the spirit of the land and water. In Cambodia, Naga often appear on temples and bridges.

GIANT CATFISH OF THE MEKONG

Perhaps the legendary Naga are really giant catfish. The Mekong River is known to be home to the Mekong giant catfish, the largest freshwater fish in the world, weighing as much as 340 kg (750 lbs) and measuring up to 2.7 m (9 ft) in length. Sadly, the giant catfish population has declined radically during the last 20 years.

NAGA FIREBALLS

Every year during the bright, autumn full moon, mysterious fireballs shoot up from the Mekong River into the sky above. Scientists have been unable to find a logical explanation. Legend has it that the Naga spit these fireballs to celebrate the end of the autumn rains. Could the legend be true?

CHAPTER 2
Bloodsuckers

The team pushed through the jungle. Charlotte was still reeling from the helicopter experience and found the intense heat and sticky humidity overwhelming.

They arrived at the base camp just as darkness fell over the trees. There they met the remaining members of the expedition: Phhoung Suy, a reptile specialist; Anthony 'Ant' Bugg, an insect expert; Seyha Dith, a spider specialist; and Bopha Sin, an expert in plants.

As Charlotte shook hands with Ant, she gasped when she saw a praying mantis sitting by his ear.

"What?" Ant asked in response.

"Do you know you have a bug on your ear?" Charlotte said with obvious revulsion.

"Oh, that's just Lorna. She showed up on my first day here and won't leave me alone."

Afterwards, he looked over at Lorna and, picking her up, said, "C'mon, Lorna. Let's get you some dinner."

"Dinner?" Charlotte said.

"He keeps a supply of insects in his cabin to feed to predatory insects like praying mantises," Seyha explained.

"You mean he chooses to live with creepy things?" Charlotte asked.

"Yeah, he loves 'em. He calls them his 'friends'," Seyha continued, rolling her eyes.

Charlotte thought that was pretty 'creepy'.

After the introductions, Charlotte was finally able to take in her surroundings. She was relieved to discover that the camp was actually pretty civilised: there was a kitchen, a lab and a real toilet!

"Come on! I'll show you your cabin," Bopha said as she led Charlotte away.

"Cabin?" Charlotte thought. She was not sure she had heard correctly, but she did indeed have her very own timber cabin with a straw roof and a cot to sleep in. The cabin was on stilts so that equipment could be stored out of the rain underneath, as well as to avoid any unwelcome visitors from the jungle.

"Thank goodness!" she thought to herself. She started unpacking her things, and then Liz came over.

"Hey, don't get too comfortable," Liz said. "We're only staying here tonight. Tomorrow we have work to do, and that means we need to head deeper into the forest."

That night it was cold, and the sounds of crickets and frogs, coupled with the thought that her next night would be spent sleeping on the ground, kept her awake. In spite of this, the night seemed to pass quickly, and before the sun had even come up, Liz poked her head into the cabin.

"Time to get up! Are you ready for your adventure to start?"

"Hasn't there been enough adventure already?" Charlotte thought.

Soon they were traipsing through the thick forest of lush green ferns and tall trees. Kiri led the way, chopping plants with his machete as he pushed deeper into the wilderness. Charlotte felt the heat and humidity beginning to build up shortly after the sun had come up. All around her, she could hear the rustling of trees and countless different types of chirps, caws and calls from the birds and animals in the forest. Every once in a while, she would see geckoes or snakes vanishing beneath fallen tree trunks. The scent of wet grass filled the air, and there was not another soul to be seen.

From time to time, Charlotte would get the feeling that they were being followed. She could not explain what it was, but whenever she looked behind her, she saw only more plants and trees.

After some time, they came to a clearing with what appeared to be a long path snaking into the distance. Kiri pointed out some large, round tracks, and explained that this path was an elephant corridor, a trail used by elephants when they migrate. Charlotte wondered if she would get to see an elephant during this trip.

Charlotte continued to take in all of these new sights and sounds, amazed and fascinated by everything she was seeing, hearing and smelling. She often found herself scanning the forest, hoping to spot a tiger. She knew she might never see one – they are extremely endangered and usually only come out at night.

Unfortunately, the mosquitoes were amazed and fascinated by her, too, and had decided that they liked her more than they liked everyone else. It felt as though she were being eaten alive by the little bloodsuckers, even though she had covered herself with insect repellent from head to toe. Her feet were also covered in painful blisters, and she was sweating so much that she thought she might never dry out.

Kiri tried to cheer Charlotte up by offering her some berries he had picked and was snacking on. Charlotte was not very convinced that the berries would be very

tasty but followed Kiri's directions to be polite. As it turned out, she was right: they were a bit sour for her taste. She nevertheless consoled herself with looking at the beautiful butterflies that surrounded her – lemon emigrants and striped blue crow knights.

The hiking continued like this for several hours. Charlotte began daydreaming about ocean breezes and ice cream, when she noticed something black on her leg. On her return to reality, she realised that it was a leech! She screamed loudly and fell down on the ground. Her face was white in panic.

Kiri came over to see what was wrong and let out a deep chuckle. "And here I thought it was something really serious," he told Charlotte.

"You don't think this is serious!" she exclaimed. "What should I do?"

"Well, whatever you do, don't rip it off. Leeches release a substance that makes blood flow more quickly when they're drinking and then let out another chemical that slows the flow when they're finished. If you tear the leech off before it's done, you'll bleed all over the place."

Charlotte felt as though she was going to be sick.

Kiri giggled. "Just leave it alone. It will drop off once it's had its fill."

This gave Charlotte little comfort, but she tried to compose herself and got up to continue with the hike. As Kiri had predicted, a few minutes later, the fattened leech dropped off into the grass.

How has the author conveyed Charlotte's reaction to the leech?

Animals of the Cardamom Mountains

Asian elephant

Asian elephants have smaller ears than African elephants and have had a close relationship with humans for thousands of years.

Flying squirrel

These squirrels come out at night and can extend their arms and legs to create a parachute with their bodies.

Clouded leopard

Clouded leopards are the smallest of the big cats. They are excellent at climbing trees, and their markings are perfect camouflage in the forest.

GREAT HORNBILL

This bird is the largest member of
the hornbill family and is named
after its huge yellow bill.

250 cm/100 in.

200 cm/80 in.

MALAYAN SUN BEAR

This small bear uses its teeth
and extremely long, curved
claws to climb trees.

150 cm/60 in.

SIAMESE CROCODILE

Long thought to have
become extinct in the
Cardamom Mountains,
the Siamese crocodile
was rediscovered in 2000.

100 cm/40 in.

50 cm/20 in.

0 cm/0 in.

41

How to Avoid Bites and Stings

The most dangerous animals are not tigers, bears or crocodiles; they are much smaller creatures that bite, sting or transmit nasty diseases. You will need to know how to avoid these – and what to do if you are hurt!

MOSQUITOES

THE DANGERS

Millions of people suffer from diseases carried by tropical mosquitoes. These include yellow fever, the West Nile virus, dengue fever and malaria.

WHAT TO DO:

- use insect repellent on your skin
- always sleep under a mosquito net
- use mosquito-repellent candles and other devices.

ANTS

THE DANGERS

Many of these live in large colonies, which they defend by swarming over intruders and biting or stinging them.

WHAT TO DO:

- stay away from nests
- get medical help fast if you suffer multiple stings or if any of the stings are inside your nose, mouth or throat.

SNAKES

THE DANGERS

Most snakes are not venomous at all, but some can be deadly. Cambodia has many venomous snakes, including cobras and vipers.

WHAT TO DO:

- wear sturdy boots
- use a stick to tap the ground in front of you to ward off snakes
- if someone is bitten, seek medical help immediately and keep the affected area below the level of the victim's heart.

SPIDERS

THE DANGERS

Nearly all spiders are venomous. Luckily, very few are able to bite humans, but some spiders are very dangerous. There are many venomous spiders in Cambodia.

WHAT TO DO:

- avoid places where spiders might live
- carefully check clothing and footwear
- if you are bitten by a spider, seek medical attention fast.

OTHER DANGERS

Avoid ticks by wearing long trousers and sturdy boots.

Check clothes and footwear carefully to avoid scorpions.

CHAPTER 3
Up Close and Personal

They continued hiking through the hot, wet forest for a few hours. Every time it seemed as though they might stop, someone would say something like, "Nah, there are too many trees here," or "The streams are too far away." At one point, Charlotte thought she heard Phrun snickering at her exasperation, and she started to wonder whether everyone was doing it just to tease her.

Finally, Liz addressed the group. "This looks like a good spot. What does everyone else think?" They were in a wide clearing surrounded by trees, and they could hear the trickle of a stream nearby. The birds chirped blissfully around them. Everyone agreed with Liz's judgment – especially Charlotte.

It was late in the day, so Liz suggested they just set up camp and take it easy until the next day. Charlotte was relieved to hear this.

Charlotte began setting up her sleeping area. She unpacked a hammock, a canvas covering called a flysheet, a mosquito net and a folding chair. Then she noticed Phrun busily setting something up – and it was not a hammock. She asked Liz what he was doing. Liz explained that he was setting up a camera trap, which consisted of a camera that would be triggered if an animal walked in front of its lens. This would enable Phrun to capture pictures of the more elusive nocturnal animals.

Charlotte smiled to herself. Pictures of night-time animals sounded awesome.

She continued with her sleeping arrangements, installing the hammock first. She found two sturdy trees a reasonable distance apart and tied either end of the hammock to them. Next she tied the mosquito net over the hammock to keep the little bloodsuckers out, followed by the fly to keep the rain away.

Finally, Charlotte unfolded the chair next to the hammock and placed her backpack on it. This was a tip she had learned in her jungle training sessions: possessions should never be left on the ground because the forest dew would make them soaking wet by morning – or maybe some creepy-crawlies might tuck in for a nap inside! She was very proud of herself for paying attention and remembering.

After a dinner of curry and rice with the group, Charlotte decided she was too exhausted to stay up any longer and headed straight for bed. She put her boots on the folding chair, took a blanket out of her bag, and moved to sit casually and gently on the edge of the hammock. She barely made contact with it, however, as it slipped out from under her, and she fell hard on the soft, soggy ground.

Ant had been hanging out with his bug 'friends' nearby and, seeing what had happened, burst out laughing in a loud guffaw. Charlotte could not help but giggle a little, too.

Fortunately, she was more careful the next time around, and after changing into dry clothes, she found that her second attempt was more successful.

During the night, the rains resumed, and Charlotte was soothed by the sound of rain droplets on the fly. The night was cold and pitch black. The density of the tree canopies and the thick cloud above them obscured the stars and moon completely. She enjoyed her best night's sleep in days.

In the morning, after breakfast, she dressed for a day of surveying in the jungle. She began putting her boots on, first her right boot, and then her left. Just as she put her left foot in the boot, she felt something wriggle at the sole of her foot. She yanked her foot out with a quick motion and screamed. Everyone in the camp came running over to see what it was.

Charlotte pointed at her boot,
and Phrun went over to take a look.
He glanced inside the boot and smiled.
He put his hand in and pulled out
a very long, thin green snake.
Charlotte was speechless. Phrun saw
her expression
and said,
"It's a young
vine snake. It didn't
bite you, did it? Vine snakes
are highly venomous."

What words would
you use to describe a
night in a jungle?

Charlotte felt the blood rush down from her head to her body. She had turned as white as a sheet, when Phrun continued, "I'm just kidding! Vine snakes are not very harmful. They are pretty cute, though," he said, looking googly-eyed at the snake.

Phhoung butted in, "How marvellous! Vine snakes are a fascinating species. Instead of laying eggs as most snakes do, they give birth to live young. Vine snakes live in trees, so it is very unusual for them to be found near the ground. I wonder what attracted this one to your boot."

Liz chimed in, "It's just one of many amazing snakes found in the Cardamom Mountains. A few years ago, they

discovered a whole new species of wolf snake here. Maybe we'll get to see one!"

Phrun looked at Charlotte and smiled. "We're such shameless nerds," he shrugged. "On the topic of nerdiness, though, you should come and check out the photographs my camera trap took."

His photographs were fantastic – there were a serow (a goat-like animal), an Asian golden cat, a family of porcupines, a sambar deer and even a tiger! "Maybe I'll get to see a tiger in real life!" Charlotte thought.

Cardamom

22 November, 2002

NEW SNAKE SPECIES DISCOVERED IN CARDAMOM MOUNTAINS

By Ally LeCroc, Science Editor

RARE WOLF SNAKE, *LYCODON EFFRAENIS*, FOUND IN CAMBODIAN HILLS.

A species of wolf snake has been recorded for the first time in the Cardamom Mountains, according to findings to be published in the December issue of *Herpetologica* magazine.

Wolf snakes are non-venomous and are identified by their wolf-like teeth, where most other snakes have fangs.

Courier

Herpetologists Jennifer C. Daltry and Wolfgang Wüster first discovered the unusual snake on a boulder near a forest stream while conducting a survey of the wildlife in the Cardamom Mountains in the year 2000.

They have named it *Lycodon cardamomensis*, or the Cardamom Mountains wolf snake.

Daltry and Wüster explained that, although they had only found one specimen, its unique characteristics convinced them that it must be a new species. The Cardamom Mountains wolf snake has a distinctive pattern of six well-defined, broad, white bands across the tail and six across the black body.

Until recently, the region was relatively unexplored, but the lush forests of the Cardamom Mountains are now gradually being depleted by logging and slash-and-burn farming. As a result, the Cardamom Mountains wolf snake will be included on the Red List of Threatened Species by the International Union for the Conservation of Nature (IUCN).

A concentrated effort to survey the biodiversity of the Greater Mekong region – of which the Cardamom Mountains is a part – is under way.

Fellow herpetologist Dr. Newt Cayman said of the find, "This is an exciting discovery, and it's only the beginning. New species are being discovered here all the time, but it's a race against time to document all of the species and ensure they are protected before they are lost forever."

Getting Ready for Bed

If you have to spend the night out in the jungle, a fly-and-hammock combination is the best type of shelter. This arrangement will provide plenty of ventilation and keep you dry. Here is how to set it up.

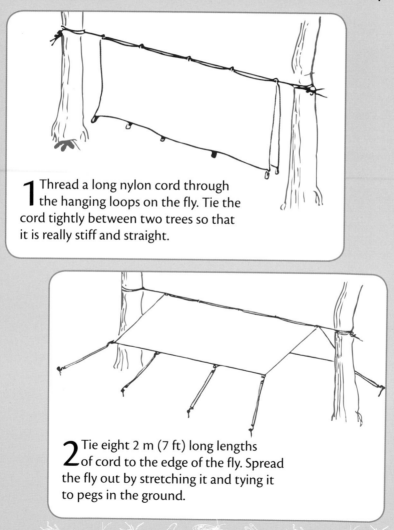

1 Thread a long nylon cord through the hanging loops on the fly. Tie the cord tightly between two trees so that it is really stiff and straight.

2 Tie eight 2 m (7 ft) long lengths of cord to the edge of the fly. Spread the fly out by stretching it and tying it to pegs in the ground.

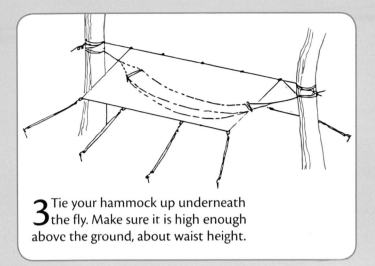

3 Tie your hammock up underneath the fly. Make sure it is high enough above the ground, about waist height.

4 Tie the mosquito net up above the hammock and below the fly. Fit a thin, 1 m (3 ft) stick onto the net at either side to create a box shape. Tuck the mosquito net into the hammock to create a totally enclosed space.

NOW GET INTO THE HAMMOCK, BUT TRY NOT TO FALL OUT THE OTHER SIDE!

Nocturnal Animals

SLOW LORIS >

This loris gets its name from its slow speed. Lorises have gripping hands that are great for climbing through trees, and big eyes so they can see at night easily.

< PALM CIVET

Striped bushy-tailed palm civets are able to live in a range of habitats. They mostly live in trees but sometimes look for mice and insects on the ground.

YELLOW-THROATED MARTEN >

These brightly coloured animals have very long tails and eat fruit and small animals. They are not shy and are known for their unpleasant smell.

❮ MALAYAN PANGOLIN

Pangolins are covered in scales, which act as both body armour and camouflage. They have no teeth and collect food (ants and termites) with their long tongues.

ASIAN LEOPARD CAT ❯

Leopard cats are about the size of house cats but are thinner and have longer legs. They come in many different colours but are recognisable by their leopard-like spots.

❮ MALAYAN PORCUPINE

Like other porcupines, Malayan porcupines are covered with black-and-white quills. They eat plants and insects and are often found in pairs.

CHAPTER 4
Bugs, Bugs, Bugs!

One day early in the expedition, Seyha invited Charlotte to join her and Ant on a foray into the forest to set up a canopy fog. They set off from the camp, each carrying a backpack full of equipment. Charlotte did not have a clue what any of it was or how it worked, but she was sure she would soon find out.

After a few minutes – they were still within sight of the camp – Seyha suggested they stop and set up the canopy fogging area. Seyha put some rope over her shoulder and began effortlessly climbing a nearby tree. The speed at which Seyha ascended made Charlotte wonder if, while working with spiders all these years, she had been bitten by one and gained spider-like superpowers like Spider-Man – Seyha was like a spider-woman!

Once Seyha had reached a high branch, she flung the rope over it and dropped both ends down to Ant. There below, he caught them and tied one end to a piece of equipment, which looked like a box with a tube attached to it.

Ant began pulling the other end of the rope until the box reached the branch Seyha was sitting on. She grasped it and placed it on the branch next to her, tying it securely to the tree.

Meanwhile, Charlotte helped Ant to arrange several funnel-shaped containers on the ground below. Within a few moments, Seyha was climbing back down the tree just as easily as she had scaled it a few minutes before.

Once Seyha was on the ground, Ant pulled a radio transmitter out of his bag.

"So, how does this work?" Charlotte asked, with genuine interest.

"Once we flick the switch on the radio transmitter here, the fogger up there will release a chemical that will confuse any insects or arachnids (spiders) in the tree," Seyha explained. "In this confused state, they won't be able to hold on to the tree or their webs, and they will drop down into these funnels. Once there, we can record what species there are, what they look like, and how many there are of each type. Then we'll pack everything up, move to another tree, and start all over again."

"Doesn't it hurt the bugs?" Charlotte asked, worried.

"No, their bodies are pretty tough and can handle the impact. And the effects of the chemical are temporary. The little creatures will soon be back to normal."

"Oh, good," Charlotte replied without thinking about it.

"So, are we ready?" Ant asked.

"Yep, ready!" came Seyha's response. "Now we wait."

After about half an hour, something finally clicked inside Charlotte's brain: it was about to start raining bugs!

"Uh, I think I might head back to camp now," Charlotte announced.

Seyha nodded, but Ant paid no attention to her. Charlotte managed to get away just as what seemed like hundreds of insects and spiders began falling from the tree into the funnels. She was relieved to see that none of them landed on Seyha or Ant.

"Although Ant probably wouldn't have minded!" she mused. She was even more relieved that she was nowhere near them.

As she looked away from Seyha and Ant, she caught sight of a sudden movement out of the corner of her eye. Her head turned in the direction of the activity. It was a tiger! Her heart jumped. She watched as the tiger creeped towards a small deer.

Just as Charlotte was about to turn away to avoid witnessing the deer's violent end, she saw it leap to safety. Relieved, her mind next turned towards the coincidence of seeing a tiger again.

"Could it be the same tiger?" she wondered, excitedly. If she had taken a better look at it, she would know, since no two tigers have the same markings.

She headed back towards camp in a daze of excitement. She had seen a tiger in real life! Nearing the camp, she heard a commotion. She saw Kiri running towards the sound and decided to head over to see what was going on, too. When she arrived, she saw Bopha lying on the ground, clearly in great pain.

"What happened?" Charlotte asked.

"Bopha slipped on some rocks and broke her leg. We had to radio for an emergency evacuation," Kiri responded.

A few minutes later, she heard the rhythmic sound of helicopter blades. It became louder and louder until a large, red-and-white aircraft finally arrived.

Robin signalled to the pilot using hand gestures. Unfortunately, there was nowhere for the helicopter to land, so the pilot had no choice but to keep hovering above, while a medic abseiled out of a side door.

Inside the helicopter, another person lowered a stretcher and a black case down to the medic. The medic yelled over the sound of the helicopter's whirring blades. "How is she doing?"

"She says she's doing OK, but I think she's in a lot of pain," Robin said.

After doing a few checks on Bopha, the medic said to Robin, "Can you help me get her onto this stretcher?" Robin nodded.

"Ready? One. Two. Three!" Robin and the medic lifted Bopha onto the stretcher. Next the medic strapped her on and gave a signal to the other person in the helicopter. Soon Bopha was being lifted into the air and pulled inside the helicopter. The medic was lifted up too, and then the helicopter flew away into the distance.

As she watched the helicopter disappear, Charlotte thought, "I certainly hope Bopha will be OK."

Then, as if she had read Charlotte's thoughts, Liz said, "Don't worry. I'm sure Bopha will be fine."

What words would you use to make the rescue more dramatic?

Rescue Helicopter

Main rotor blade provides lift

Main rotor hub controls blade pitch angle to climb or descend and turn the helicopter

Windshield with panoramic visibility

Ventral window for view of landing area

VHF blade aerial for radio communication

Landing skid of high-strength steel

Helicopters are very useful for scientists going on expeditions to remote areas. Here is a type of helicopter that is often used in search and rescue operations and medical evacuations.

Tail rotor prevents fuselage (body) from spinning and gives low-speed rudder control

N120HH

Tail boom of carbon fibre or aluminium

Vertical fin provides high-speed directional control

Hide and Seek

Insects are all around us, but many are so well camouflaged that they are hard to spot. With the help of a tray and a piece of white paper, you can bring them out into the open.

WHAT YOU WILL NEED:
shallow tray
white paper
scissors
stick
magnifying glass

WARNING!
Always ask an adult for help when using sharp scissors.

1 Cut a piece of white paper to fit the bottom of your tray. Line the tray with the paper.

white paper

shallow tray

2 Place the tray under a leafy branch and tap the branch with the stick so you can see the insects tumble out.

magnifying glass

3 Use the magnifying glass to get a close-up view of the insects as they fly or crawl away. Try using the tray under different plants to see which bugs live where.

IMPORTANT: Do not pick up any of the bugs you collect because they may bite or sting – or you might hurt them! Let them crawl or fly back to where they came from.

Helicopter Hand Signals

Helicopters make too much noise for their pilots to be able to hear instructions from people on the ground. Instead, they rely on hand signals, such as these.

I AM YOUR
SIGNALLING GUIDE

START ENGINE

HOVER FACING ME

LOWER A LITTLE

UP A LITTLE

MOVE RIGHT

MOVE LEFT

TAKE OFF

LAND

STOP ENGINES

CHAPTER 5
Down by the River

Most days, the expedition team split up to observe and record animals they saw in the forest near the campsite. Some days, they ventured further. On one such day, Charlotte joined Liz, Phhoung and Finn on an excursion to explore the fish, reptile and amphibian life in the nearby river. It always made Liz feel sad to think that the Siamese crocodile had become extinct in this region. When she heard that it had been rediscovered, she was relieved – and excited. Today she was hoping to see if she could spot the Siamese crocodile for herself.

It had been raining almost non-stop since they arrived, so they were all wearing rain ponchos. They took some inflatable rafts with them and headed towards the river. Upon arrival, they unpacked and inflated their rafts. They paddled upstream until they reached a wetland at the foot of a hill, and Finn suggested this might be a good spot to explore. The rain stopped just as they arrived, much to everyone's relief, and they all disembarked and tied their rafts to trees.

As Liz and Finn took notes on the animals that they saw in the murky water, Charlotte helped Phhoung to set up traps and nets.

Afterwards, they all decided to break for lunch. They enjoyed a meal of canned sardines, crackers and fresh fruit that Kiri had gathered in the forest the day before.

"Mmm. Such a good selection of fruit! This finger banana is so sweet, and this mangosteen has such a wonderful texture. We're really spoilt here," said Finn.

"Well, it certainly makes a change from canned ham and oat crackers," said Liz.

"I think the sweetness of the rambutans complements the richness of the sardines," Charlotte commented.

Everyone looked at Charlotte in surprise. They looked at each other and burst out laughing.

"Yes, it's a real gourmet feast we have here," said Finn, chuckling.

They continued to eat in silence for a while, and then Charlotte commented, "Is it just me, or does it seem like the river is flowing a bit faster? Doesn't it look dirtier, too? Eww, it's turning brown, and it's full of twigs and leaves."

Finn's eyes opened wide and stared at Charlotte with alarm. He looked over at the water, and, as if a light switch went on inside his head, he yelled, "Quick! Get up the hill! NOW!"

What was funny and surprising about Charlotte's comment?

No one bothered to ask why – everyone followed his instructions immediately.

Just as they reached the summit of the hill, an enormous torrent of water came rushing down the river. The water was frothy and brownish in colour; it carried mud, leaves and the occasional tree branch. The group seemed to be safe on the hill, though.

"What happened?" said Charlotte, completely out of breath.

"Flash flood," replied Finn gravely. "We got out of the way just in time."

"What do we do now? Are we going to get rescued like Bopha?" asked Charlotte.

Finn answered calmly but seriously, "We simply need to sit tight and wait it out. The water level will go down in a couple of hours, but we'll probably need to abandon the survey for today. If there are any animals left around here, they won't be the ones that live here normally."

"It must have been caused by all that rain," announced Phhoung.

"Yes. We should have been more alert," Finn agreed. "Flash floods often follow heavy rainfall. At least we managed to get out of the way in time. That certainly was a lucky escape!"

Charlotte could not believe what had happened. They could have all drowned!

Soon the water seemed to reach its peak, and they all settled down to wait for it to recede. They played I Spy to pass the time.

"I spy with my little eye something that begins with T," Charlotte began.

"T-shirt!" said Finn. Charlotte shook her head.

"Twigs!" said Liz.

"Trees!" said Phhoung, laughing.

"No, tiger!" said Charlotte. She looked over at another hill nearby. Everyone followed her line of sight. There, totally undaunted by the gushing water, was a big, orange tiger with black stripes and a white belly. It was watching the water, and then it looked over at the group of scientists.

"Hey! A tiger! He looks so comfortable over there. I guess we should just take our cue from him and relax for a while," said Liz.

Charlotte smiled back, and returned her gaze to the tiger on the nearby hill. "Could it be the same tiger?" she wondered.

A few hours later, the water receded, as Finn had predicted. Having lost the rafts, they packed up all of the supplies that they had rescued and followed the river's path back downstream towards the camp.

CARDAMOM DISPATCHES

ABOUT ME

My name's Charlotte, and I'm a student training to become a biologist. I decided to join my mentor Liz on a scientific expedition to the Cardamom Mountains of Cambodia. This is my blog about it. My likes include sleeping, fashion, and most of all, animals (especially big cats!)

DAY 20
28 September
CARDAMOM MOUNTAINS

There's never a dull moment in the Cardamom Mountains. I've already told you about the helicopter emergency landing, hiking through the jungle, seeing spectacular and beautiful plants and animals, leeches, mosquitoes, the snake in my boot, the camera trap photos, the canopy fogging and Bopha's medical evacuation! I didn't think our expedition could get any more exciting, but wait until I tell you what happened next.

Liz was desperate to find a Siamese crocodile, so she, Finn, Phhoung and I headed upriver to observe the animals that live in and near the water. We saw a lot of amazing creatures — tons of different frogs and fish, including bullfrogs and catfish. While we were eating lunch, I noticed that the water was turning a darker colour and that there were lots of leaves and branches in it. That's when Finn told us to get out of the way – it was a flash flood! We made it to a safe place on top of a hill just in time. It really was close!

The flood meant that we didn't manage to see the crocodile. We saw something else, though: on another hill nearby, I saw the last thing I expected to see – a tiger! He was just lying down on a big rock, as if nothing was happening! He was so beautiful.

Before coming on the expedition, I had really hoped I would get to see a tiger. I knew I might not, because tigers are extremely rare. I certainly didn't expect to have three sightings! I wonder if all three are the same tiger. I feel so lucky. This trip's turning out to be such an amazing experience. I can't wait to see what happens next!

Fruits of Cambodia

Visit a Cambodian market, and you will be able to experience a range of exotic and delicious fruits. They are excellent in salads or alone as a snack.

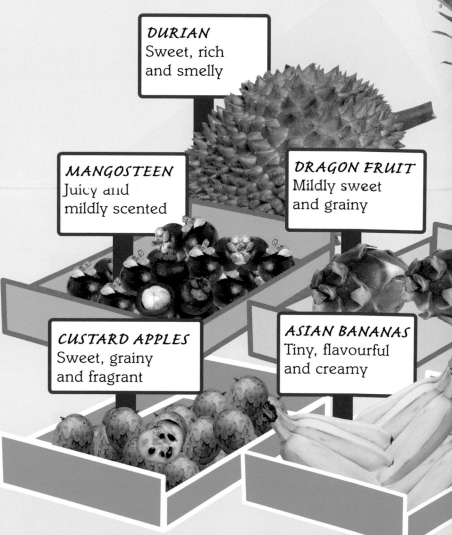

DURIAN
Sweet, rich and smelly

MANGOSTEEN
Juicy and mildly scented

DRAGON FRUIT
Mildly sweet and grainy

CUSTARD APPLES
Sweet, grainy and fragrant

ASIAN BANANAS
Tiny, flavourful and creamy

PINEAPPLE
Tangy and
refreshing

**GREEN
COCONUT**
Rubbery
and sweet

GUAVA
Sweet, sharp
and juicy

RAMBUTANS
Mild, juicy
and sweet

PAPAYA
Smooth and
fragrant

CHAPTER 6
Rescue Me

Most days, Charlotte would join a few members of the team on walks in the forest to set up traps for animals and to see what they could find. Then they would release the animals unharmed. Over the course of several weeks, they saw pileated gibbons (a kind of ape), clouded leopards, gaurs (bison), moustached hawk cuckoos, silver orioles and many other mammals and birds.

One day Charlotte rose early from her hammock and recruited Liz, Robin and Phrun for just such a walk. After many hours of walking, recording and setting traps, they heard something in the distance. "ROARRR! GRRROWL! ROARRR!"

Phrun gasped. "I think it's a tiger! Sounds like it's getting into a fight!" Without really thinking about it and probably against his better judgment, he began running in the direction of the sound. Charlotte, Liz and Robin chased after him.

Phrun arrived at a clearing but stopped short, his eyes staring at something in disbelief. Robin, Charlotte and Liz caught up with him and saw what was so disturbing to him. They were not prepared for what they saw: in the clearing stood a tiger with his foot caught in a wire attached to a tree. The wire was so tight around his foot that it had started to dig into the tiger's skin, exposing the red flesh underneath. The tiger roared and growled in distress and flailed side to side in a desperate attempt to free himself. "ROARRR! GRRROWL! ROARRR!"

Charlotte stood watching motionless and speechless, dizzy with confusion and incapable of working out what to do. Phrun was furious. "How can people do this?" he yelled in frustration. "It's so cruel. As if tigers don't have enough problems, terrible people come and try to trap endangered animals to sell their body parts to the highest bidder. It's disgusting!"

"You mean someone did this on purpose?" Charlotte whispered to Liz.

"Sadly, yes. It's illegal to trap endangered animals like this, but people make so much money from selling them and their parts that they risk it," Liz explained.

"So they trap animals just for the money?" asked Charlotte in disbelief.

"It's not just greed," Liz continued. "People who live in these rural communities are very poor. Sometimes it's the only way they can think of to make money to pay for food and shelter for their families. Ultimately, however, they make very little money, and it is actually the powerful people they work for who benefit the most."

Charlotte could not believe what she was hearing. She was starting to understand why Phrun was so angry. Robin went over to Phrun to try to calm him down.

"Phrun, at least we found him before the poacher did. We can help him. Let's radio the forest rangers to come and get him."

The muscles in Phrun's face and shoulders began to relax when he heard Robin's words. "You're right," Phrun said. "Let's call for help."

Liz and Robin hurried back to the camp to radio the rangers, while Phrun and Charlotte stayed behind to make sure the poacher did not swoop in. Phrun and Charlotte waited in silence, lost in thought. The tiger had stopped growling, too, as he lay down on the ground uneasily.

Liz and Robin did not take long and soon returned. "The rangers are on their way. They said it might be a few hours before they can reach us, though."

It seemed like a long time, but nobody could think of doing anything other than waiting.

"So, have you seen this kind of thing before?" Charlotte asked warily.

"Unfortunately, yes," replied Robin. "The illegal wildlife trade is a really big problem, especially in this part of the world. This kind of thing happens far too often."

After a while, they heard some rustling and the sound of breaking twigs coming towards them. A group of about twelve men was approaching, carrying a stretcher and a large case.

As they neared the clearing, the tiger stood up. "GRRROWL! ROARRR!" The men barely blinked. Phrun spoke to them for a few minutes and then announced, "They're the rescue team. They're going to sedate the tiger and take him away."

One of the men was holding what looked like a rifle. He raised it up and aimed at the tiger.

"NO! What is he doing?" Charlotte exclaimed, worried.

"Don't worry, Charlotte," Liz said. "That gun just shoots tranquilizer darts. It's the only way to help the tiger without getting mauled!"

A dart went into the tiger's neck. He slumped and fell to the ground. He began breathing heavily as if he had fallen asleep. Two other men set about cutting the snare off with wire cutters while carefully avoiding hurting the tiger any further.

Another man sprayed the wound thoroughly with antiseptic.

Next they were ready to put the tiger on the stretcher. It took everyone's help to get the 200-kilogram animal onto it. The twelve men got into formation around the stretcher. After a few words of farewell and thanks, they lifted the tiger and carried it away.

As the team watched them trudge through the forest, Charlotte asked, "What will they do with the tiger?"

Phrun replied, "They'll load the tiger into their truck and take him to Phnom Tamao Wildlife Rescue Centre, an hour outside of Phnom Penh. They'll keep him there until his wounds heal and then bring him back here so he can return to the wild."

"Oh, good. I'm glad at least some people are looking out for him," said Charlotte.

How You Can Help

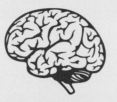

BE INFORMED

Find out as much as you can about endangered animals and their habitats. If you are well informed, you can better spread the message to others that endangered animals need our help.

HELP CONSERVATION ORGANISATIONS

Sponsor an animal through a wildlife organisation, such as Wildlife Alliance (www.wildlifealliance.org), or protect an acre of land through Conservation International (www. conservation.org), which has helped to protect the Cardamoms since 2002. Donations will support conservation of the forests and species like the ones described in this book.

There are many ways to help look after animals and the forests. Here is how to get started.

GO GREEN

Help to prevent climate change. Reduce the amount of greenhouse gases, such as carbon dioxide, that is released into the air as a result of the things people do. Reuse, repair or recycle things instead of throwing them away. Save energy by turning off electricity when it is not needed. Walk, cycle or take public transportation instead of the car.

PROTECT FORESTS

Buy wood products certified by the Forest Stewardship Council (FSC). This means that the wood is from forests that are carefully looked after to prevent losing too many trees or harming wildlife or local communities.

TIGERS

If you are like Charlotte and love tigers, find out more about how to save them at Save Tigers Now (www.savetigersnow.org).

Tiger Fact File

Tigers are the largest cats in the world. Sadly, they are endangered, which means that there are very few of them left. The two biggest threats to tigers are hunting and deforestation – both caused by humans. There are now only about 3,200 tigers living in the wild.

- **HEIGHT:** 60 cm–1.1 m (2–3½ ft)
- **LENGTH:** 1.4–2.8 m (4½–9¼ ft)
- **WEIGHT:** 100–300 kg (220–600 lb)
- **SPEED:** up to 65 kph (40 mph)
- **RANGE:** India, Thailand, Nepal, Bhutan, Malaysia, Russia, Bangladesh, Indonesia (Sumatra), Myanmar, China and Lao PDR

A tiger's tail hangs loosely when relaxed and twitches when nervous or agitated.

An average litter is two to three cubs, which weigh about 1 kg (2 lb) each at birth.

TIGERS LIKE WATER AND OFTEN SWIM IN POOLS TO COOL OFF.

No two tigers have the same pattern of stripes.

Tigers hunt at night; they can see well in the dark.

A tiger's roar can be heard up to 3 km (2 miles) away.

Tigers sneak up on their prey and then pounce, using their teeth and claws to pull the animal down.

CHAPTER 7
One More Time

The team had now been living in the forest for over a month. Charlotte had gotten used to sleeping in the hammock and getting up early. She was also becoming quite an expert on the animals of the forest and how to find them. She even knew where and how to gather fruit in the forest and which plants could be eaten.

The expedition was coming to an end. There was less than a week to go before they would all have to pack up and leave. They had recorded dozens of species in the forest and in the nearby stream – sun bears, flying squirrels, buffy fish owls, greater mouse deer and catfish, among others – but they had not yet ventured upriver again since the flash flood had interrupted their earlier research. Liz still had not managed to see the Siamese crocodile.

"Maybe we'll never find any," she said early one morning. "The Siamese crocodile might be as hard to find as the Naga in the Mekong River. Maybe I should just be satisfied with what I've already seen and accept that I probably won't ever see one."

Charlotte did not normally question Liz's ideas, but this time she could not help but disagree.

"No. We can't give up so easily! Maybe we just haven't been looking in the right place! I say we try going upstream again. If we hurry, we might be able to get up there before it starts raining again!"

Liz was silent for a minute. When Liz spoke, there was a complete change in her tone. "You're right! What am I thinking? I don't know what came over me. We have to go back!"

She hurried over to tell Finn and Phhoung about their plan. Less than an hour later, they were all packed and ready to go. Once again, they walked over to the stream where they had been conducting most of their research. They inflated their rafts, hopped in and headed upstream.

They stopped even further away than they had before, in an area where a couple of streams broke off from the river. They disembarked and tied their rafts to trees.

Once again, the group set up traps and nets in the river and surrounding streams and sat down on the riverbank to record what they saw.

They studied the streams for several hours, not even bothering to stop for lunch, munching instead on some crackers while they watched. After some time, Charlotte noticed something floating in the water. It was moving slowly, forming large ripples. Her eyes and brain were tired from having watched for so many hours, and she did not comprehend what she was seeing at all. After several minutes, she realised it must be a species she had not noticed before. She thought she could see an eye and tried to get Liz's attention.

"Liz!" she whispered. "Look over there. Is that something new? What is it?"

Liz glanced over to where Charlotte was pointing and did a double take. Quickly, she grabbed her camera and frantically started taking photographs. She could barely contain her excitement.

"Are you taking notes on this?" Liz asked Charlotte ecstatically.

"Notes on what? What is it?" said Charlotte impatiently.

"That Siamese crocodile over there. That's it! We've found it!" she whispered.

She looked back at it with wide eyes. She could not believe they had actually found it! She was so happy.

"I told you we'd find it," Charlotte said, with a wink.

That's when they noticed another crocodile lying on the riverbank. After a few minutes, the crocodile on the riverbank crept into the stream and disappeared just as the other one had.

"Pretty exciting, eh?" said Liz. She stood up to tell Finn and Phhoung what they had just seen and suggested that they all check the traps and nets and then call it a day. Everyone agreed.

Charlotte, Finn and Liz began inspecting their traps and nets. At each trap, they took notes on what they found; afterwards, they set the animals free and packed up the equipment.

They continued checking the traps and recording what they saw. They also took notes on any tree frogs they came across. Liz was calling out the names of the species she saw. "Striped spadefoot froglet, East Asian bullfrog, crowned bullfrog...."

All of a sudden, she noticed something and paused: "... Hey, now. Who's this little fella? Hmm. I'm not sure what this one is. He looks a bit like a Smith's frog, but his markings are a bit different." She took some photos of the tiny frog and put him back in the stream.

Before long, they had finished checking all the nets and had packed everything up. They climbed back into their rafts and headed downriver.

"Hey! No flash flood this time," said Finn "What a disappointment!"

Everyone stared at him gravely and then burst out laughing.

"Yes, I suppose it was a little less eventful," Liz said as she looked over to Charlotte and smiled.

"No, not eventful at all," Charlotte replied sarcastically.

Why does Finn call the team's second trip upstream 'a disappointment'?

Meet the Experts

PEPPER WILDE: *Hello! And welcome to* Meet the Experts. *I'm Pepper Wilde. Today we're speaking to three scientists who've just returned from an expedition counting the animals in the Cardamom Mountains of Cambodia – Liz Terrapin, Anthony Bugg and Phrun Keo. Welcome!*

LIZ TERRAPIN: *Thank you for having us.*

PW: *So, why exactly were you counting the animals?*

LT: *By counting the animals, we can see whether any of them are in danger of extinction, whether those that were endangered aren't anymore, and if there are any new species we need to start looking after. All of this helps us to plan how we can help animals. It also tells us how our planet as a whole is doing because animals are the first ones to know when something isn't right with the Earth.*

PW: *What made you decide to do the survey in Cambodia?*

ANTHONY BUGG: *The Cardamom Mountains are rich with rare wildlife, much of it endemic, meaning that it only exists here. This is also an area that has not been explored much and needs to be studied.*

PW: What was it like out there?

LT: Amazing and beautiful. It's so peaceful. There are no other people, just lots of fantastic animals – birds, butterflies, lizards, snakes, frogs, monkeys...

PHRUN KEO: It's really hot and humid, too! You're sweating all the time. It's definitely an adventure, though – full of surprises!

PW: What was the best part of the trip for you?

LT: Seeing a species I hadn't seen before! People are discovering new species in the Cardamoms all the time, but it was still a big thrill for me!

PK: For me, it was getting some awesome pictures from my camera trap. Camera traps are a great way to capture photos of animals because there are no people around to scare them away. Animals just act normally, so we took some fantastic pictures of porcupines, deer and a tiger.

PW: Would you do it all again?

LT: Definitely!

AB: Absolutely!

PK: In a heartbeat!

Welcome to Phnom Tamao Wildlife Rescue Centre

The Phnom Tamao Wildlife Rescue Centre is run by the Cambodian Forestry Administration, with support from the Wildlife Alliance, an organisation that aims to protect wildlife and their habitats. At Phnom Tamao, more than 1,200 rescued animals are cared for, and ultimately returned to the wild if possible. No animal in need is ever turned away.

Chhouk's story

Chhouk, a young Asian elephant, has a prosthetic foot. He was found as a baby, wandering the forest alone. He had lost his foot in a poacher's snare, and the wound was infected. Wildlife Alliance cared for him in the forest for two weeks, before transporting him to Phnom Tamao. Chhouk is now healthy again and walks around on his prosthetic foot as if nothing happened.

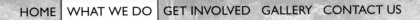

Meet the animals

Phnom Tamao is home to a range of animals who will be happy to welcome you. Come and meet them!

Epilogue

Two weeks after Liz and Charlotte saw for themselves that the Siamese crocodile did indeed live in the Cardamom Mountains, they and a few other members of the expedition team rewarded themselves with a bit of tourism. They visited the ancient ruins of Angkor Thom, Angkor Wat and Ta Prohm near Siem Reap to the north of the Cardamom Mountains.

The sites were huge, magnificent and surrounded by jungle. The group spent several days exploring monumental sculptures, hidden passageways and magnificent temples. Ta Prohm was Charlotte's favourite. The trees growing through its stones reminded her of something one of her teachers had once said: "As soon as humans complete a building, nature gets to work pulling it down."

As they walked through the ruins, climbing over tree roots and enormous stones, Liz and Charlotte discussed the 44-day expedition.

"I started evaluating everyone's results last night," said Charlotte. "I calculated that we recorded 28 species of ant, 20 species of cricket, 33 species of fish, 32 species of reptile (including the Siamese crocodile), 21 species of amphibian and 45 species of mammal. And I think your mysterious frog might be a new species."

"Charlotte! You shouldn't be working! It's time to relax," Liz replied. There was a moment of silence, and then Liz added, "You really think it might be a new species?"

Charlotte nodded. "Yeah. I checked the database and even sent our data to the lab. They think it might be a new species, too."

Liz smiled, and Charlotte smiled back at her. Charlotte was so proud to have been a part of such an important expedition.

As they reached the top of the Central Sanctuary of Angkor Wat, they looked down over the surrounding forest.

Liz interrupted the silence, saying, "I wonder how that tiger we rescued is doing. Do you think he's OK? Maybe we could go to visit him at Phnom Tamao."

At that moment, Charlotte noticed something orange and striped moving through the trees. It stopped, and Charlotte could just about make out its yellow eyes gazing back at her.

Charlotte replied, "You know what, Liz? Something tells me he's OK."

Allow yourself to be transported back to an enchanting and mysterious ancient world with Naga Tours. Our three-day Angkor itinerary will guide you through the dense jungle to the ancient capital of the great Khmer Empire.

CAMBODIA

Angkor Thom

Ta Prohm

Angkor Wat

DAY 1: Angkor Wat

Begin with a visit to Angkor Wat at sunrise. The largest religious monument in the world, 'Angkor Wat' literally means 'the City that is a Temple'. Built during the 12th century by King Suryavarman II, this spectacular complex was originally dedicated to the Hindu god Vishnu. It became a Buddhist sanctuary in the 13th century.

DAY 2: Angkor Thom and the Bayon

Spend your second day at the ancient Khmer city of Angkor Thom, which means 'Great City'. Founded by King Jayavarman VII in the late 12th century, it was the largest city in the Khmer Empire at one time. The most famous site in Angkor Thom is the Bayon, a temple with more than 200 huge stone faces.

DAY 3: Ta Prohm

Finish your tour by taking in the spectacular Ta Prohm. Perhaps best known as the temple from *Tomb Raider*, it was a Buddhist monastery built during the reign of King Jayavarman II. Now covered with the sprawling roots of giant banyan trees, it may be the most mysterious of all the temples at Angkor.

Jungle Quiz

See if you can remember the answers to these questions about what you have read.

1. What is Liz hoping to see on the expedition?

2. Why does Liz say that a helicopter is the best way for the team to get where they are going?

3. What technique do people living near the Cardamom Mountains use to clear land?

4. What kingdom of living things do humans belong to?

5. Which real-life animal might be the legendary Naga?

6. What kind of 'dinner' does Ant keep for his praying mantis Lorna?

7. Why does Charlotte think she might not see a tiger?

8. By whom do the mosquitoes seem to be 'fascinated'?

9. What does Phrun set up when the group arrives at the campsite?

10. What happens when Charlotte first tries to get into her hammock?

11. Which reptile was discovered in the Cardamom Mountains in 2000?

12. What kind of Cambodian animal is covered with body armour?

13. What does Charlotte see on another hill during the flash flood?

14. How much does the average tiger cub weigh at birth?

15. Why does Anthony say in his interview that the Cardamom Mountains are a good place to look for animals?

Answers on page 125.

Glossary

Antiseptic
Substance used for preventing infection.

Atmosphere
The layer of air that surrounds the Earth.

Audible
Able to be heard.

Compose
To calm down.

Deforestation
The destruction of forests.

Dispatch
A report sent by an expedition team.

Ecstatically
With excitement.

Elusive
Difficult to find.

Endangered
In danger of disappearing completely (becoming extinct).

Fertile
Able to grow many healthy crops.

Fragrant
Having a pleasant smell.

Habitat
The area where an animal lives.

Humidity
Amount of water in the air.

List
To tilt sideways.

Machete
A knife used for cutting large plants.

Nocturnal
Active at night.

Predatory
Hunting and eating other animals.

Sedate
To calm down with medication.

Survey
To gather information about something.

Undaunted
Not worried.

Index

Answers to the Jungle Quiz:
1. The Siamese crocodile; **2.** Because there are few roads;
3. Slash-and-burn technique; **4.** Animals; **5.** The Mekong
giant catfish; **6.** Insects; **7.** They are endangered and
nocturnal; **8.** Charlotte; **9.** A camera trap; **10.** She falls out;
11. The Cardamom Mountains wolf snake; **12.** A pangolin;
13. A tiger; **14.** 1 kg (2 lb); **15.** They have many unique
animals and have not been explored much.

Guide for Parents

DK Reads is a three-level interactive reading adventure series for children, developing the habit of reading widely for both pleasure and information. These chapter books have an exciting main narrative interspersed with a range of reading genres to suit your child's reading ability, as required by the National Curriculum. Each book is designed to develop your child's reading skills, fluency, grammar awareness, and comprehension in order to build confidence and engagement when reading.

Ready for a *Reading Alone* book

YOUR CHILD SHOULD

- be able to read independently and silently for extended periods of time.
- read aloud flexibly and fluently, in expressive phrases with the listener in mind.
- respond to what they are reading with an enquiring mind.

A VALUABLE AND SHARED READING EXPERIENCE

Supporting children when they are reading proficiently can encourage them to value reading and to view reading as an interesting, purposeful and enjoyable pastime. So here are a few tips on how to use this book with your child.

TIP 1 Reading aloud as a learning opportunity:

- if your child has already read some of the book, ask him/her to explain the earlier part briefly.
- encourage your child to read slightly slower than his/her normal silent reading speed so that the words are clear and the listener has time to absorb the information, too.

Reading aloud provides your child with practice in expressive reading and performing to a listener, as well as a chance to share his/her responses to the storyline and the information.